The Story of
BRITAIN'S BLACK AIRMEN

K. N. Chimbiri

Illustrations by
Elizabeth Lander

■SCHOLASTIC

Contents

Chapter 1: Britain in the Early 1900s.............7

Chapter 2: Alexander Patterson.................10

Chapter 3: The First World War.................15

Chapter 4: William Robinson Clarke............18

Chapter 5: The Birth of Britain's Royal Air Force...23

Chapter 6: Between the World Wars.............26

Chapter 7: Britain Calls.......................32

Chapter 8: Errol Barrow......................38

Chapter 9: Cy Grant..........................42

Chapter 10: Ground Crew......................46

Chapter 11: John Henry Smythe 50

Chapter 12: No More War 55

Chapter 13: Twice Forgotten 58

Chapter 14: Cy Returns to Holland 62

Glossary *66*

Selected Bibliography *68*

Photo Credits *68*

Acknowledgements *69*

Index *70*

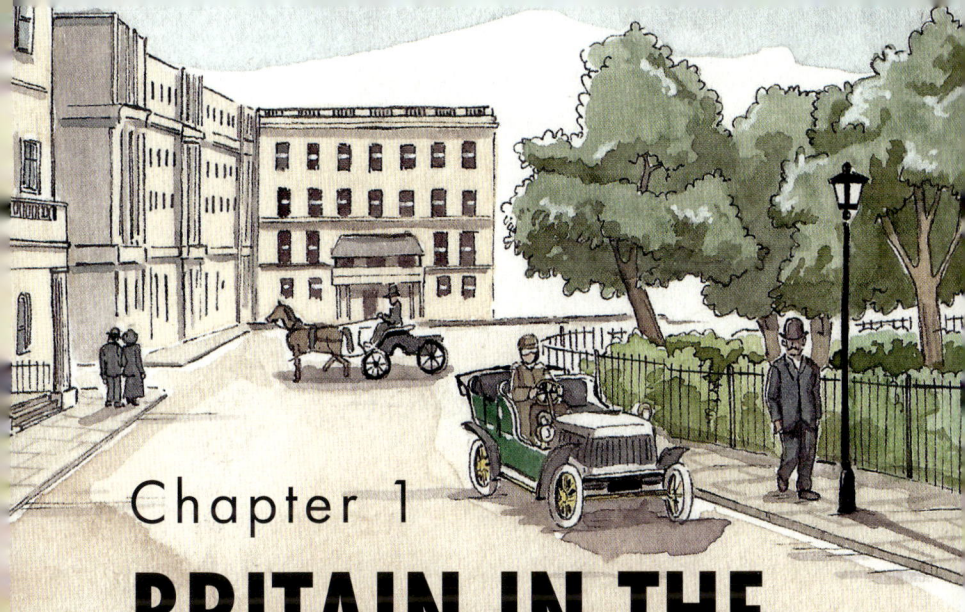

Chapter 1
BRITAIN IN THE EARLY 1900s

At the turn of the century, Britain was a rich and powerful country. However, not everyone in the country shared in this great wealth. British society was divided by a class system. People belonged to the class their parents belonged to. It was a strict system and it was difficult to move into another class if you were not born into it.

The upper classes enjoyed huge wealth and power. The middle classes included doctors, lawyers and shop keepers. The lower classes, which most people belonged to, worked as coal miners, labourers and servants.

As well as class divisions, society did not see men and women as equal. Whether they belonged to the upper, middle or lower classes, women were expected to get married, have children and look after the home. People of all classes usually accepted that men from the upper classes were their leaders.

Britain's wealth came from its **natural resources**, such as coal, and from its **empire**. Britain's huge empire gave it control of all the minerals and crops in its colonies around the world. Raw materials like palm oil, rubber, sugar, cotton, gold, tobacco and tea were sent to factories in Britain. Workers in Britain made these raw materials into **manufactured** goods which were then sold in Britain and around the world, including in the British colonies, at a **profit.**

Most people in Britain at this time were white British. Even though they were all white British people, the upper and middle classes were taught that people from the lower classes were not as good as them. They often employed the lower classes as servants to do their cooking and cleaning. The lower classes in turn were taught to believe that upper and middle class people were their 'betters'.

Britain had built up its empire over hundreds of years. The people in the lands claimed as **colonies** outside of Europe were not, in the main, white. The British colonizers travelled around

the empire taking their ideas about class and gender with them. They didn't usually make friends with the local people in their colonies. Over time white British people developed ideas about people who were not white. These ideas about **race** were added to the existing ideas about class and gender.

Because Britain was at the centre of a huge and rich empire, over the centuries, people would sometimes arrive there from different parts of the world. These people, usually men, sometimes came alone to study or they came by working as seamen on ships. Sometimes they stayed in Britain and married local white British women. Over time, Black and mixed-race Black communities developed near seaports in cities like Cardiff, Liverpool, Glasgow and London's East End. They weren't big communities and most white British people had never met or seen a Black person in real life.

Chapter 2
ALEXANDER PATTERSON

Britain's First-Known Black Pilot

The age of flying began when the Wright brothers made their successful flight at Kitty Hawk in the USA on 17 December 1903. At the time, an 11-year-old boy called Alexander Patterson lived far away across the Atlantic in England.

Alexander had been born in February 1892 in the port city of Southampton on the south coast of England.

Alexander's father was a Black man from the British colony of Barbados. He worked as a seaman. Alexander's mother, Emma, was a white English nurse who had worked for three years for the British Royal

Above *Photo of Alexander Patterson's father taken in London, 1888*

Right *Alexander Patterson, 1892–1962*

10   THE STORY OF BRITAIN'S BLACK AIRMEN

Family in St James's Palace in London. Alexander's parents were married at St Margaret's Church, Westminster. At first, they lived with Emma's mother in her house in a wealthy part of Belgravia in London. Later on, they moved to Southampton where Alexander's father continued to work at sea.

When Alexander was a teenager he started working for shipbuilding companies in Southampton, as well as helping to check the goods that came into the Southampton docks. Alexander was also studying to become a **mechanical engineer**. In 1913, when he finished his five years of studies, Alexander applied to join the new **Royal Flying Corps (RFC)**.

The Wright brothers' flight in the USA had only taken place ten years earlier so flying was still a new and exciting science. In Britain, the RFC had just been formed (in 1912) to train pilots and test aeroplanes for both the British Army and the Royal Navy.

Alexander's technical skills were valuable. He was given a job as a mechanical **draughtsman** at the RFC's headquarters in Farnborough in Hampshire. And shortly after he joined the RFC, on 7 July 1913, he was promoted to First Class Air Mechanic. To be a part of the new RFC was really something! People admired the men who were working with the new flying machines.

Chapter 3
THE FIRST WORLD WAR

1914 to 1918

Alexander had been serving in the RFC as a First Class Air Mechanic for about a year when, on 4 August 1914, Britain declared war on Germany. Alexander was soon sent to France and in October that year he was promoted to Corporal. He was at the First Battle of Ypres (*ee-pruh*). Ypres is a town in Belgium near the French border. Heavy fighting took place near the town over several weeks and huge numbers of men on both sides were killed. Alexander survived and in January 1915 he was promoted again, this time to Sergeant.

A few months later, on 19 July 1915 Alexander gained his Royal Aero Club certificate and then he became a qualified pilot. Although it wasn't Alexander's main job to fly the planes, he still had to accompany the men who were learning to become pilots. This was so he could teach them what sounds to listen to in their engines when they were in the air.

After Alexander had been in France for almost a year, he was sent back to England and continued to serve in the RFC. He was soon promoted again … twice! (His first promotion was to Flight Sergeant and then Sergeant-Major.)

As he was promoted, Alexander became a type of officer known as a non-commissioned officer (an NCO).

There were commissioned and non-commissioned officers. A commissioned officer had a higher **status** than an NCO. Commissioned officers wore uniforms made of better fabric, ate better food and were allowed to go to the officers' mess (a place where the commissioned officers could relax, eat and drink together).

Because of the strict class system in Britain and its empire, commissioned officers were expected to come from the upper middle and upper classes.

Men from the lower classes sometimes became commissioned officers but it wasn't common. Instead, they might become NCOs, like Alexander did, by 'working their way up through the ranks'. This meant if they did a good job there was a chance they might be promoted.

And, because of the ideas about race at the time, men who were not white were not supposed to become commissioned officers at all. So it's quite amazing that, in October 1917, Alexander was chosen to become a commissioned officer, with the rank of Second Lieutenant.

Chapter 4
WILLIAM ROBINSON CLARKE

Britain's First-Known Black Combat Pilot

When the First World War started, many white men in Britain and throughout the British Empire wanted to **enlist**. At least forty-two white men from Trinidad and Tobago came to Britain and joined the RFC. Several white men came from Jamaica and the other Caribbean colonies too. Some of the white Caribbean men who joined the RFC became pilots.

But it wasn't just the white men from the colonies who wanted to fight for Britain during the First World War. Thousands of young Black men were just as eager to 'fight for King and Country'.

Right *William Robinson Clarke, 1895–1981*

Some Black men in the colonies wanted to fight for Britain because they felt it was their duty as **citizens** of the British Empire. Others wanted to escape the poverty of Britain's colonies and see more of the wider world. Some people thought that Britain would be grateful for their help and might even reward their colonies with more political rights and better social conditions.

William Robinson 'Robbie' Clarke from Jamaica was working as a **chauffeur** for a wealthy family when the First World War started. Robbie wanted to join the RFC. He managed to get enough money to pay for his own fare to travel to Britain. In 1915 he sailed from Jamaica with his friend Lancelot 'Lance' Alexander McIntosh who was also going to England to **volunteer**. When Robbie arrived, he went to the RFC headquarters in Farnborough and asked to join.

Like Alexander Patterson, Robbie had important and, at that time, rare skills. He knew how to drive and he knew how to fix cars. Few people in Jamaica, or in Britain, could fix or even drive a car. Cars were so expensive in the early twentieth century, that only the middle and upper classes could afford them. Working-class people could never own one. They could only stop and stare as wealthy motorists drove past them.

Robbie came to Britain with letters praising his skills. The letter writers were several of the professional men and motor experts from Kingston, the capital of Jamaica. Like Alexander Patterson, two years earlier, Robbie was allowed to join the RFC. He was sent to France as a driver but when he saw the planes flying overhead, he really wanted to fly too. Robbie was accepted for pilot training and returned to Britain to learn how to fly. In those days, learning to fly was quite dangerous and men often died in training accidents. But Robbie survived and after four months, he became Sergeant Pilot Robinson Clarke.

At this time the RFC mainly used planes to be the 'eyes of the army'. Pilots, like Robbie, flew planes over the enemy's territory. Another airman, called an **observer,** wrote notes and took photographs of enemy **troop** locations, movements and weapons.

Although they weren't fighting below in the **trenches**, flying was still a dangerous job. Planes were small, flimsy, propeller-driven **bi-planes** with open **cockpits**.

Robbie's plane was shot up at least six times. Then, on 28 July 1917 while flying over the **Western Front:**

'I was doing some photographs a few miles the other side when about five [German] scouts came down upon me, and before I could get away, I got a bullet through the spine. I managed to pilot the machine nearly back to the aerodrome, but had to put her down as I was too weak to fly any more […] My observer escaped without any injury.'

Robbie managed a **pancake landing**. He was badly wounded, but he survived. After he recovered from his injuries, Robbie continued to work for the RFC although he didn't fly any more operations (missions).

Chapter 5

THE BIRTH OF BRITAIN'S ROYAL AIR FORCE

The Royal Flying Corps lasted from 1912 to 1918. In its earliest days, when Alexander Patterson joined, it helped both the British Army and the Royal Navy. Then, in July 1914 part of the RFC broke away to become the Royal Naval Air Service (RNAS). So, during the First World War, the RNAS helped the navy while the RFC helped the army.

When the First World War was coming to an end, Britain no longer needed as many planes, pilots and other airmen. Flying was still dangerous, aeroplanes were still small, and flying hadn't

The King's Message to the Royal Air Force.

To the Right Hon. Lord Weir, Secretary of State and President of the Air Council.

IN this supreme hour of victory I send greetings and heartfelt congratulations to all ranks of the Royal Air Force. Our aircraft have been ever in the forefront of the battle; pilots and observers have consistently maintained the offensive throughout the ever-changing fortunes of the day, and in the war zones our gallant dead have lain always beyond the enemies' lines or far out to sea.

OUR far-flung squadrons have flown over home waters and foreign seas, the Western and Italian battle lines, Rhineland, the mountains of Macedonia, Gallipoli, Palestine, the plains of Mesopotamia, the forests and swamps of East Africa, the North-West frontier of India, and the deserts of Arabia, Sinai, and Darfur.

THE birth of the Royal Air Force, with its wonderful expansion and development, will ever remain one of the most remarkable achievements of the Great War.

EVERYWHERE, by God's help, officers, men and women of the Royal Air Force have splendidly maintained our just cause, and the value of their assistance to the Navy, the Army, and to Home Defence has been incalculable. For all their magnificent work, self-sacrifice, and devotion to duty, I ask you on behalf of the Empire to thank them.

November 11th, 1918   *George R. I.*

The message which King George V addressed to the Royal Air Force, through Lord Weir, Secretary of State and President of the Air Council, on 11 November 1918.

yet become a way for lots of people to travel around together like they do today. In April 1918 the two air arms (the RNAS and the RFC) joined together to become the Royal Air Force (RAF). It was the world's first **independent** air force.

The new RAF's rules were written up. And it was decided, as with the rest of Britain's Armed Forces, that men who were not of 'pure European descent' wouldn't be allowed to join the new RAF. The contributions of the early Black pilots like Alexander Patterson and Robbie Clarke were largely forgotten in Britain. Few people remembered Alexander's achievements: working his way up to become a commissioned officer and his ability to fly six different types of aeroplane.

After the war ended, Robbie was given some medals and some money, and he returned to Jamaica. Robbie was forgotten in Britain. And, although he was Jamaica's first Black pilot, Robbie's story is not very well known in Jamaica either.

While Robbie became a pilot, his friend Lance had become an observer. Lance had also been injured during the war but recovered. He became a flying instructor and taught many other men how to fly. Lance also became a commissioned officer and stayed in the new RAF until he retired in 1948. A few years later he returned to Jamaica.

Despite the rules and attitudes at the time towards people with Black ancestry, Alexander, Robbie and Lance helped Britain during the First World War and played a part in the early history of flying.

Chapter 6
BETWEEN THE WORLD WARS

After the First World War ended in 1918 there weren't many opportunities for Black men – or women – to fly anywhere in the British Empire. Flying was still an expensive sport, like motor car racing, enjoyed mainly by the very wealthy. And, because of racial attitudes at the time, people who were not white were usually unwelcome in the flying clubs in the British colonies.

Sometimes Black men from Britain's Caribbean colonies learnt to fly in the USA or Canada – like Sidney Kennard from British Guiana, Hubert Fauntleroy Julian from Trinidad and Dr Albert E. Forsythe from Jamaica.

Hubert Fauntleroy Julian became known as 'The Black Eagle of Harlem'. He sometimes flew with a pioneering female African American flyer called Bessie Coleman.

Dr Albert E. Forsythe permanently settled in the USA when he was a young man. In 1934 he flew with Charles Alfred Anderson, an African American, from the USA around

A Jamaican fighter pilot - Flight Sergeant Tucker - serving with R.A.F. Fighter Command.

the Caribbean. They flew to several countries including the Bahamas, Cuba, Jamaica, Haiti, the Dominican Republic, Puerto Rico, the Virgin Islands, Grenada, Trinidad and British Guiana.

Later on, Charles Alfred Anderson helped to train the first Black military pilots in US history. These airmen became known as the **Tuskegee Airmen**.

When Britain declared war on Nazi Germany on 3 September 1939 the rules still prevented men who were not of 'pure European descent' from joining the RAF. However, now that Britain was at war again it needed more men to help. In October 1939 the RAF changed its rules so men who were not white could now join.

The Royal Navy and the British Army weren't as accepting as the RAF, so most Black men who came to Britain during the Second World War served in the air force. In the end, about six thousand Black airmen from the Caribbean joined the RAF.

Flight Sergeant James Hyde, a fighter pilot serving with No 132 Squadron, Royal Air Force, pictured by a Supermarine Spitfire with 'Dingo', the squadron commander's pet dog, at Detling, Kent, England, December 1943. Hyde, from San Juan, Trinidad, arrived in Britain more than two years previously to commence his training.

BETWEEN THE WORLD WARS

Chapter 7
BRITAIN CALLS

William 'Billy' Strachan dreamed of joining the RAF:

'I never thought of the Army or the Navy. The next adventure on my list was to fly aeroplanes. And there were none in Jamaica.'

Although he was only eighteen years old and had just left school, Billy sold everything he had and paid his own fare from Jamaica to England. He arrived in March 1940 with £2 and 10 shillings and a suitcase containing one change of clothing. Although the rules had changed six months earlier, when Billy tried to join the RAF some of the staff turned him away at first. Billy became one of around 450 Black aircrew. He served at first in bombers as a wireless operator. After completing more than the required thirty operations, Billy retrained as a pilot and completed another fifteen trips.

Like Billy, Vincent Bunting from Jamaica made his own way to Britain. He arrived a bit later in 1940 while the Battle of Britain was taking place – a fierce struggle between the RAF and the German **Luftwaffe** to control Britain's skies.

Billy Strachan
1921–1998

Vincent Bunting

Britain had declared war on Germany in 1939 after Germany, led by Adolf Hitler, invaded Poland. Since then Germany had invaded more and more countries. By June 1940 most of Western Europe was **occupied** by Germany. Britain was the next country on Hitler's list.

Germany's air force attacked Britain. But the RAF defended Britain mostly by using its fighter planes to fight the Luftwaffe. The Battle of Britain lasted from 10 July to 31 October 1940. The RAF won and then, although they continued to defend Britain, also went on the attack against Germany using bombers.

Nearly 3,000 white men took part in the Battle of Britain as fighter pilots. Most were white British men. Some were volunteers from **neutral** countries like the USA and Ireland. Some came from the occupied European countries like Belgium, France, Poland and Czechoslovakia. Others were white men from many parts of the British Empire and **Commonwealth** including colonial Africa and the Caribbean (Barbados and Jamaica).

Although he didn't take part in the Battle of Britain, Vincent became a fighter pilot. He flew Spitfires from 1942 to October 1944. He also flew other planes later on in the war.

In 1940 the island colony of Barbados sent two small groups of men to fight for Britain. The first group left in July. These were fourteen white **Barbadian** men coming to volunteer for all parts of Britain's armed forces. The second group left Barbados in November 1940 just to join the RAF and this group included both Black and white Barbadian men. One of the Black men in the second group was a young man called Arthur O. Weekes. Arthur became a Spitfire pilot. Another young Black man in the group, Errol Walton Barrow, became a **navigator**. After the war Errol returned home and later became the first prime minister of Barbados.

Collins A. Joseph and Arthur O. Weekes

Chapter 8
ERROL BARROW

Errol was born on 21 January 1920 in the British island colony of Barbados. Errol's family were well off and they cared about helping others who were less fortunate. His family wanted to change social conditions like the racism and poverty of colonial life in Barbados.

Errol served Britain during the Second World War as a navigator. Over the years, aeroplanes had become bigger and better but, in those days, there were no computer systems that helped the pilot to fly. Instead, the navigator told the pilot where to go. It was a difficult job and the navigators were nicknamed 'the brains of the plane'.

The pilot, Andrew Cole, a white Englishman, remembered when he chose Errol to be his navigator:

'Amongst the navigators there was one handsome, six-foot, Black Barbadian, the only Black person in the room. I asked him if he would like to fly with me. We agreed to put our lives in each other's hands and became friends for life.'

Errol Barrow,
1920–1987

Errol completed forty-eight bombing operations for Britain during the war. On 4 November 1944 he became a commissioned officer and achieved the rank of Flying Officer.

After the Second World War ended in 1945, Errol worked as the personal navigator and Andrew as the pilot for Sir William Sholto Douglas. Sir Sholto was in charge of everyone who was a part of the RAF in Germany. Errol and Andrew's job was to fly Sir Sholto and his staff around in one of his planes.

When Errol left the RAF in 1947 he studied to become a **barrister**. Then he returned to Barbados in 1950 and five years later, he helped to start a new political party. Errol became known in Barbados as 'the father of **independence**'. He helped Barbados move to self-rule and became the first Prime Minister of Barbados in November 1966. Errol also improved access to education, health care and social conditions for everyone in the country.

JOIN AN AIR CREW
IN THE RAF
APPLY YOUR NEAREST COMBINED RECRUITING

Chapter 9
CY GRANT

In 1941, Cy Grant left his home in British Guiana (today's Guyana) to join the RAF. Cy dreamed of being a pilot and flying planes like Spitfires.

Although Cy's family were not poor, they couldn't afford to send him to university. In those days not many people who lived in the Caribbean colonies could afford higher education. There weren't many opportunities and Cy thought life was boring and dull. He longed to escape and the Second World War gave him the chance.

Cy was excited when he came to England and began to learn how to fly for the RAF. Soon he would be flying a Spitfire! Then Cy got some disappointing news. He wasn't going to become a pilot. Instead, Cy was going to be made a navigator for the pilots of bombers.

In February 1943 Cy became a navigator. He was also made a commissioned officer which cheered him up a bit (although he was still disappointed that he wasn't going to be a fighter pilot).

Cy Grant,
1919–2010

On 26 June 1943, after their third bombing raid on Germany, Cy and his crew were flying back to Britain. While they were flying over the Netherlands, their Lancaster bomber was attacked – first by anti-aircraft guns from the ground, then by a German night fighter. Although they managed to get away

With Ronald Hall (second from left, front row) and Cy Grant (middle, front row). At least five other men in the photo were also from the colony of British Guiana.

from the Luftwaffe fighter, the plane had caught fire. Before Cy could escape, their plane exploded and broke into pieces. Cy felt himself falling through the air.

Cy opened his parachute and landed in a field near a village called Nieuw-Vennep. The Dutch villagers were all kind to Cy. They cleaned him up and gave him some food. Then they had to hand him over to the Germans. Cy was one of thousands of RAF men who were captured and imprisoned by the Germans during the Second World War.

During his time as a prisoner Cy thought about his life. Living as a prisoner for almost two years taught him how to live with other people under difficult circumstances. He also learnt to cope with disappointment.

Cy also thought about the state of the world. He came from a country that was a colony of the British Empire. He thought about Hitler's goal to build an empire. If Hitler was wrong now, wasn't it wrong in the past too?

Cy also thought about war. He decided that war is wrong and that fighting just isn't the way to achieve peace.

Chapter 10
GROUND CREW

Taking Care of Everything

Not everyone who joined the RAF became aircrew. Most of Britain's Black airmen were **ground crew**. Sometimes they were disappointed not to be flying in planes like the aircrew.

The ground crew performed important work on the planes to keep them flying. They looked after the engines, took care of the airframe and the instruments inside the plane. Some ground crew worked as drivers. Others worked with radios or **radar** or handled the weapons and bombs.

The ground crew's work could be very dangerous. They were also sometimes hurt or killed when German bombers flew over British air bases and attacked them. Bertram Errol Burrowes, a Jamaican, died along with others when the bomb they were handling accidentally exploded.

During the war, thousands of women joined the Women's **Auxiliary** Air Force (WAAF). Some of the first WAAFs

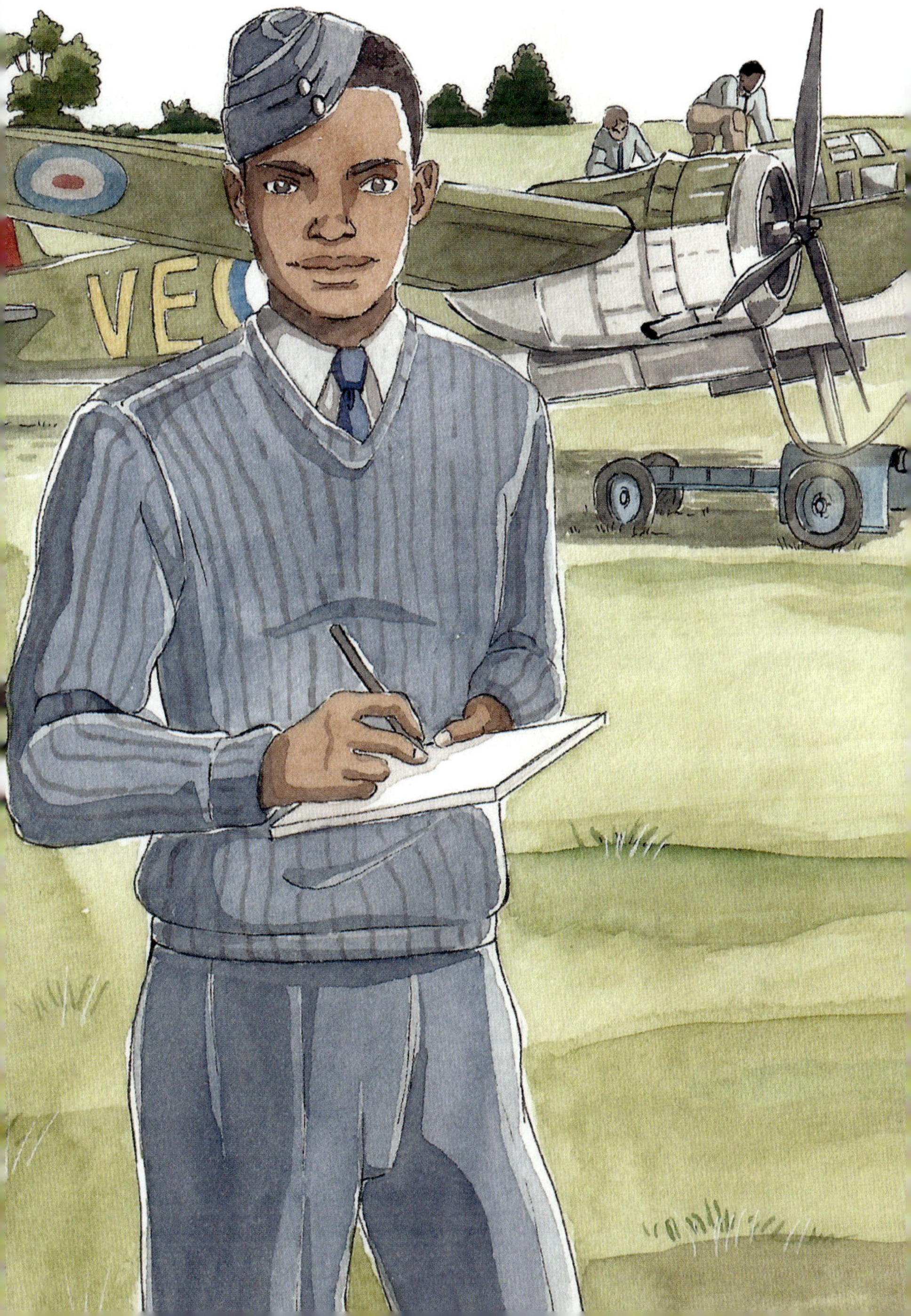
VE

came from wealthier families but as the war went on, they came 'from all walks of life'.

Lilian Bader was born on 18 February 1918 in Liverpool. Her mother was white and her father was Black. Lilian joined the WAAF in March 1941 and was one of the first women to become an Instrument Repairer. Lilian worked long hours checking the cockpit instruments for faults. She did well and was promoted to Acting Corporal.

Lilian Bader

Most of the ground crew from the Caribbean arrived from June 1944 onwards. Alford Gardner, a Black man from Jamaica, was in the first large group of ground crew to arrive. Alford served as a motor transport mechanic. These Caribbean men were Black, white, mixed race, and some were of Asian heritage (South Asian and Chinese descent).

When some of the white British airmen at the RAF base saw these 2,000 Caribbean men arriving to help them, they became quite frightened. Alford later remembered:

'They couldn't understand all these different colours, different shades of people, different nationalities, all talking the same way, and we all got on so well. Jamaicans, Trinidadians, Barbadians, Guyanese – we were all one.'

Sam King from Jamaica also worked as ground crew. He did a variety of jobs including repairing Spitfires. One of Sam's jobs was sitting alone in a radar van in the middle of the airfield helping the Mosquito fighter planes to land. He hated that job. The planes were loud and he worried that one day one of them just might land on his head.

Chapter 11
JOHN HENRY SMYTHE

Most of the Black airmen who helped Britain during the Second World War were from the colonies in, or near, the Caribbean. However, about sixty Africans also came to Britain as RAF aircrew during the war. One of them was a man called John 'Johnny' Henry Smythe.

Johnny was born in a British colony in West Africa called Sierra Leone. He volunteered for the RAF in 1940 and became a navigator. On 18 November 1943 Johnny and his crew were on their twenty-seventh mission. They were attacking the city of Mannheim in Germany when their Short Stirling bomber was shot down. Johnny was wounded. The seven men had to bail out of their plane. However, Johnny didn't land in an occupied country like Cy had. He landed right in Germany itself. Johnny and his crew were all captured by the Germans. Like Cy, Johnny was imprisoned in one of the prison camps for airmen.

After the war ended Johnny was released from the camp. He went back to Britain and worked for the Colonial Office.

John Henry Smythe,
1915–1996

Johnny was one of the African and Caribbean men who worked as liaison officers after the war ended. It was difficult for many men to get used to a normal life again after the war. Johnny's job as a Liaison Officer was to try to help the Black airmen in Britain cope with this change.

Britain's Black airmen had many of the same experiences as white British airmen. However, the Black airmen from the colonies also had to cope with being far from home. Most of them didn't have friends or family in Britain. Some white British people were kind to the Black airmen and invited them into their homes for tea or a meal so they wouldn't feel lonely and unwelcome.

Others said unkind things or picked fights with the Black airmen. During the war when white soldiers from the USA came to help Britain, they were often mean to Britain's Black airmen.

Johnny had to help them find jobs at a time when many white British people wouldn't give jobs to anyone who wasn't white. He also had to help the airmen to leave Britain and return to their homes.

After the Second World War ended, most of Britain's Black airmen went back to Africa and the Caribbean. They had to wait for **troopships** to take them. They also had to have an officer in charge travelling with them on their journey.

Johnny Smythe was the officer in charge on one of the journeys on a troopship called the *Empire Windrush*. On 8 May 1948 it sailed from Britain to the Caribbean. Hundreds of Caribbean airmen were on board, returning to their homes.

The *Empire Windrush* dropped off the airmen but it didn't return to Britain empty. There were many people who wanted to come to Britain. Some of the men like Sam King from Jamaica, who had served Britain during the war with the RAF, came back to Britain in June 1948 on this ship.

A few years after he travelled on the *Empire Windrush* from Britain to the Caribbean and back, Johnny himself left Britain. He returned to the British colony of Sierra Leone. Like Errol Barrow from Barbados, Johnny became a barrister. He became the Solicitor General for Sierra Leone and played a role when, in 1961, Sierra Leone gained independence from Britain.

Johnny later travelled to the USA giving speeches about Sierra Leone. He was in the crowd when the African-American **civil rights activist** Dr Martin Luther King, Jr gave a speech called *Let Freedom Ring* in 1963 in Washington, D.C. The speech began with the words that became famous 'I have a dream'.

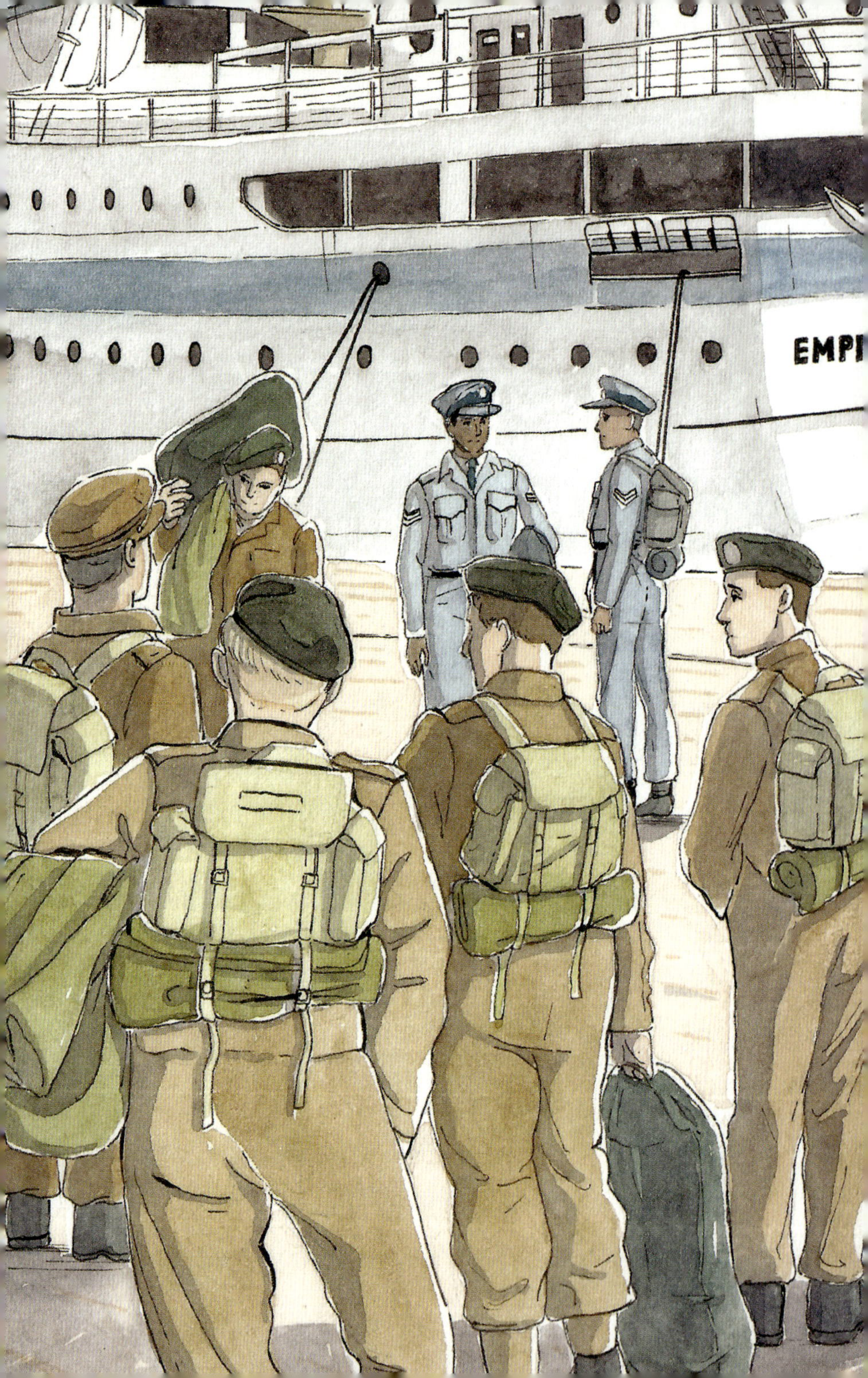
EMPI

Between 1947 and 1954 the HMT *Empire Windrush* was a troopship taking British troops to and from many ports around the world including Southampton, India, Egypt, Kenya, Yemen and Singapore.

The ship only made one journey from Britain to the Caribbean and back again (in 1948).

Chapter 12
NO MORE WAR

After the war many of Britain's Black airmen stayed on in Britain. Gilbert Clarke from Jamaica served as ground crew during the war and he remained in Britain after the war ended.

John Jellicoe Blair from Jamaica became a navigator flying in Halifax bombers. He became a commissioned officer and received the Distinguished Flying Cross (DFC). John had a

Flight Lieutenant John Blair, DFC (1919–2004)

good experience in the RAF and remained in the RAF until 1963.

Some airmen went back to their home countries but later returned. Sam King came back to Britain from Jamaica in June 1948 on the *Empire Windrush*. He later became involved in politics and in 1983, Sam became the first Black mayor of the Borough of Southwark in London.

Billy Strachan returned to Jamaica but then came back to Britain again. Like Johnny Smythe, after the war, he worked for the Colonial Office as a Liaison Officer. He later became an important Black British civil rights activist, writer, and a lawyer.

Many of the airmen who left Britain after the war ended went on to help other countries.

Ulric Cross from Trinidad also volunteered to join the RAF. He became a navigator and a commissioned officer. Ulric flew eighty missions during the Second World War. He received medals: the Distinguished Flying Cross (DFC) and the Distinguished Service Order (DSO). Ulric reached the rank of Squadron Leader. After the war, Ulric studied law and became a barrister. He used his legal skills to help Ghana, Cameroon and Tanzania. Ulric became a High Court Judge in Trinidad, then, in 1990 he became the High Commissioner for Trinidad and Tobago in London. Trinidad and Tobago was by this time no longer a British colony.

Lincoln Orville Lynch from Jamaica served as an air gunner. He shot down a German aircraft on his first mission. Lincoln was awarded the Distinguished Flying Medal (DFM) for his courage under fire. He also became a commissioned officer which was rare for an air gunner. After the war, Lincoln eventually settled in the USA and became active in the **Civil Rights Movement**.

Cy Grant remained in Britain after the war. He decided to study law so he could help people. In 1950 he became a qualified barrister. But Cy felt that it was the racism in Britain at the time which stopped him finding legal work. So, although he didn't want to, he became an actor and a singer instead. He acted on stage and in film, and sang in concert and cabaret. He also worked to help Black actors get better treatment in Britain.

Chapter 13
TWICE FORGOTTEN

During the war in Europe, people from many different backgrounds had to work together to defeat Nazi Germany, Italy and the other **Axis powers**.

After the war ended, not everyone who helped was remembered in movies or books. Britain proudly remembered the white aircrew of the fighter planes. People appreciated that they defended and protected Britain especially during its 'darkest hour' by shooting down the German bombers that were sent to destroy Britain's cities.

However, the aircrew of the British bombers were not praised much after the war. Many people were uncomfortable with how badly German cities were damaged, and by the deaths of ordinary people of all ages in bombings.

In the USA, it was different. After the Second World War ended, the all-white crews of the bombers and the fighter pilots who helped to win the war were celebrated. At first, most

V-E DAY!
Last German Units Yield
in Europe Over
Full Surrender
WAR IS OVER
IN EUROPE

Two bomber aircrew, Sergeant J Dickinson from Canada and Sergeant F Gilkes from Trinidad.

Americans knew nothing about the Tuskegee Airmen, who fought in the Mediterranean. Then, in the 1950s and 1960s there was a Civil Rights Movement in the USA. Over the next decades the Tuskegee Airmen's story was told in newspapers, magazines, and books for adults and children. There were also films, museum exhibitions and an official website to honour their legacy. Their story became better known, not just in the USA, but in the UK. Today many people in Britain know more about the first Black pilots in US military history than the story of any of Britain's Black airmen!

Even in the Caribbean and Africa, the Black airmen were largely forgotten too. People were thinking about other things like the right to rule their own countries and improving their poor conditions. They wanted independence *from* Britain, not to celebrate people who had fought *for* Britain.

Sergeant Lincoln Orville Lynch

Chapter 14
CY RETURNS TO HOLLAND

When Cy Grant fell out of the sky over the Netherlands in June 1943 Joost Klootwijk was an 11-year-old Dutch boy who lived in the village. Joost heard so many confusing stories about the crash. He kept wondering what had really happened. So, when he was older, Joost decided to learn more about what happened to Cy and all the other airmen in the burning plane that had broken into pieces above his village.

Joost spoke to people in and around his village to learn what they remembered about the crash. There was no internet, mobile phones or email in the late 1970s when Joost began his hard work. He had to write many letters to people in Britain, Holland and Canada. Joost wrote down everything he found out and it was later published as a book.

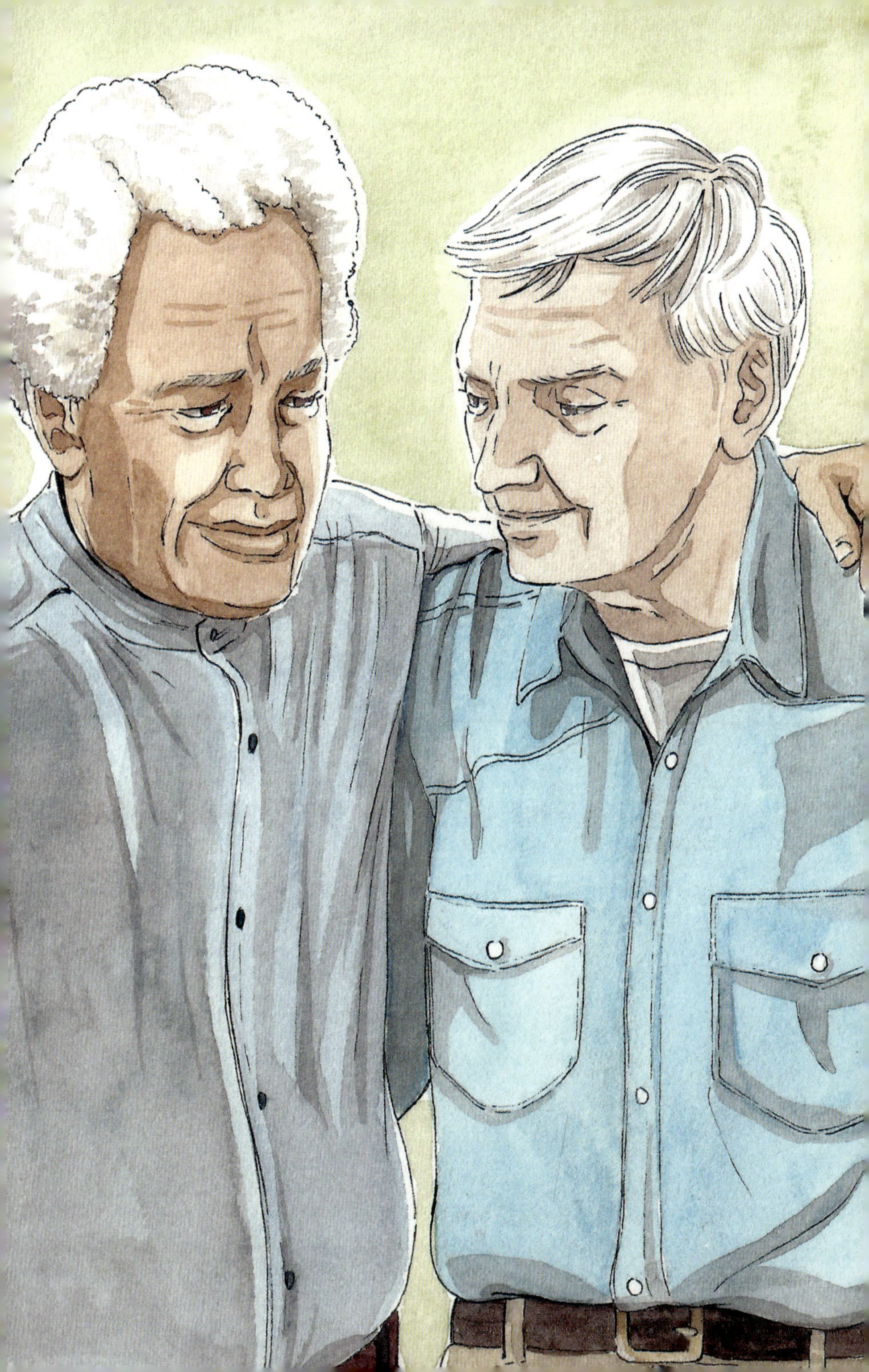

Cy had also written a short book about his time in the RAF. He wanted to remind people in Britain that Black people, like him, served in the RAF during the Second World War. Cy wanted people to learn about the past although he didn't want people to **glorify** war.

Finally, in 2008 Cy returned to Holland to see the village where he had been shot down sixty-five years earlier. And, he met Joost.

Cy received a warm welcome. Even though Britain did not want to remember the bomber crews, in many countries in Europe, like Holland, they are largely regarded as heroes who bravely tried to help rescue the occupied countries from the Nazis. Joost's son, Hans, suggested they start a website to record the names of all the forgotten Caribbean aircrew who helped Britain during the Second World War. To this day, stories about all Britain's Caribbean flyers, whether or not they were Black, are added to the website.

Britain's Black Airmen are a part of history. Despite the attitudes at the time, they were among some of the first people in the world to fly and help to maintain aeroplanes.

When the Second World War ended many of Britain's Black airmen played a role on the ground too by fighting against injustice and racism. Their lives are an important part of the fight for human rights and freedom. By aiming for the skies, many of them helped to bring about changes that are still making our world a better place.

Glossary

Auxiliary A person whose job supports the armed forces but isn't directly engaged in hostilities.

Axis powers A collective term for all the countries on the same side during the Second World War. Headed by Nazi Germany, Italy and Japan, but also included Slovakia, Romania, Hungary, Croatia and Bulgaria.

Barbadian A person who is a citizen of Barbados. See also *citizen*.

Barrister A lawyer who helps people with court cases.

Bi-plane A plane which has two wings fixed one above the other.

Chauffeur Someone whose job is to drive an important or wealthy person around.

Citizen A person from a country or empire.

Civil Rights Activist A person who strives to secure rights and fair treatment for others. In the UK, Black civil rights activists fought to end racial discrimination. See also *Civil Rights Movement*.

Civil Rights Movement A movement is a group of people with shared aims who want to see a certain change or development take place. In the USA, African Americans fought to end legal segregation and obtain fair treatment under the United States Constitution. See also *Civil Rights Activist*.

Cockpit The part of a plane where the pilot sits and flies the plane.

Colony A land that is under the control of a powerful person, country or government. See also *empire*.

Commonwealth At the time of the Second World War, some countries that were former British colonies.

Draughtsman A person who makes plans and drawings of machines.

Empire A group of lands or colonies under the control of one powerful person, country or government who conquered them. In 1900 Britain had a large empire. See also *colony*.

Enlist To join the armed forces. See also *volunteer*.

Glorify To praise, admire or honour something.

Ground crew The people who repair and maintain aeroplanes.

Independence Freedom from control by another country. See *colony*.

Independent Not controlled by an external force.

Luftwaffe The German word for their air force.

Manufactured Making raw materials into finished goods in factories.

Mechanical engineer A person who designs and tests mechanical products and systems.

Natural resources Minerals, crops and other materials that people can use to make things.

Navigator A person on the plane who had to know the plane's position at all times.

Neutral A country that doesn't take sides during a war.

Occupied countries Countries invaded and controlled by another country's armed forces.

Observer A person on the plane who had to look out to gain information about the enemy's troops, movements and weapons.

Pancake landing An emergency landing where the plane is flopped straight down.

Profit The money left over after the expenses involved in manufacturing and selling the products have been deducted. See also *manufactured*.

Race A way of grouping people together because of their shared physical features.

Radar Stands for Radar Direction and Ranging. A system that uses radio waves to locate objects like incoming bombers.

Royal Flying Corps Forerunner of Britain's Royal Air Force (RAF).

Status A person's position in society or in an organization.

Trenches A series of long and narrow ditches dug deep in the ground where soldiers lived.

Troops Soldiers or other armed forces.

Troopship A ship that transports troops in wartime or in peacetime.

Tuskegee Airmen The first African Americans to fly aeroplanes for the US military. They trained near Tuskegee, Alabama in the USA.

Volunteer To choose to join (enlist) the armed forces. See also *enlist*.

Western Front A front is a war zone where fighting takes place. During the First World War the Western Front was the main battle zone in Western Europe.

Selected Bibliography

Books

Lancaster W4827: Failed to Return. Epilogue for a Commonwealth Crew of a RAF Bomber in World War II by Joost Klootwijk, Lilliput 2008.

A Member of the RAF of Indeterminate Race: World War Two Experiences of a West Indian Officer in the RAF by Cy Grant. ISBN 978-1-846830-18-1

Caribbean Volunteers at War: The Forgotten Story of the RAF's 'Tuskegee Airmen' by Mark Johnson. ISBN 978-1-399010-16-0

Documentary films

Into the Wind, Electric Egg Ltd 2011

Flight W4827: 'Cy Grant meets Joost Klootwijk', produced & directed by Kurt Barling for BBC London News.

Websites

www.caribbeanaircrew-ww2.com

Quotes

Chapter 4: 'Jamaican is Wounded While Flying in France' in The Gleaner, 7 September 1917

Chapter 7 Strachan: Page 20 *Lest We Forget, The Experiences of World War II Westindian Ex-Service Personnel* by Robert N. Murray. ISBN 978 1 870518 52 7

Chapter 8: *'The Beautiful Blonde in the Bank'* by Flight Lieutenant Andrew Leslie Cole AFC RAF (unpublished, at bajanthings.com)

Chapter 10: Alford Gardner, *'The Story of an RAF Recruit and Windrush pioneer'*, Interview, 4 December 2017, africansinyorkshireproject.com

Photo Credits

Page 10 Courtesy of Rex Patterson

Page 24 © Imperial War Museum (CH 8949)

Page 28 © Imperial War Museum (CH 5312)

Page 29 © Imperial War Museum (CH 11978)

Page 36 © Imperial War Museum (CH 11976)

Page 44 Courtesy of Pip Jager (Ron Hall's partner) and David Gleave of www.historycalroots.com

Page 48 © Imperial War Museum (HU 53753)

Page 56 Courtesy of Sarah and John Blair

Page 60 © Imperial War Museum (PL 10348D)

Page 61 © Imperial War Museum (CH 12263)

Page 62 Courtesy of Hans Klootwijk

Acknowledgements

This book is dedicated to Uncle Carl.

I would like to express my deepest gratitude to Mrs Audrey Dewjee for her support, encouragement and patience with my numerous questions. Thank you for reading the draft manuscript, pointing out my errors and making suggestions. I'm also grateful to Tony Warner for his suggestions which have greatly improved the text. Despite this wealth of expertise, any errors or omissions in the book are solely mine.

Many others have also helped along the way with valuable pieces of information, introductions or feedback on parts of the manuscript. I'd like to acknowledge Kurt Barling, Hans Klootwijk, Lucy-May Maxwell, Samantha Moxton, Rex Patterson, Eddy Smythe and Iyamide Thomas.

Finally, I'd like to thank all my supportive friends and family, in particular, my sister Amanda and my friends Angel, Dee, Lorna and Ricky.

Index

Africa 35, 50, 52, 61

African Americans 26, 53, 66–7

Anderson, Charles Alfred (pilot) 26, 28

Bader, Lilian (ground crew) 48

Barbados 10, 31, 35, 37–8, 40, 53, 66

barristers 40, 53, 57, 66

Barrow, Errol (navigator/barrister/PM) 37–41, 53

Blair, John Jellicoe (navigator) 55–6

British Empire 8–9, 16, 18, 20, 26, 35, 45

British Guiana 26, 28, 30–1, 42, 44

Bunting, Vincent (fighter pilot) 32, 35

Canada 26, 61–2

Caribbean 18, 26, 28–31, 35, 42, 48, 50, 52–3, 55, 61, 64

chauffeurs 20, 66

citizens 18, 66

Civil Rights Movement 53, 56–7, 61, 66

Clarke, Gilbert (ground crew) 55

Clarke, William Robinson (combat pilot) 18–23, 25

class structure 7–9, 16–17, 20

Coleman, Bessie (pilot) 26

colonies 8–10, 18, 20, 26–7, 30, 35, 38, 42, 44–5, 50, 52–3, 57

Cross, Ulric (navigator/barrister/judge) 56–7

Empire Windrush 53–5

enlisting 18, 66–7

fighter pilots 28–9, 35, 42, 58

First World War 15–18, 20, 23, 25–6

Forsythe, Albert E. (pilot/doctor) 26

Gardner, Alford (ground crew) 48–9

Germany 15, 21, 28, 32, 35, 40, 44–6, 50, 57–8, 66–7

Grant, Cy (pilot/barrister/actor/singer) 42–5, 50, 57, 62–5

ground crew 46–9, 55, 67

Holland 62–4

independence 40, 53, 61, 67

inter-war period 26–31

Jamaica 18, 20–1, 25–6, 28, 30, 32, 35, 46, 48–9, 53, 55–7

Julian, Hubert Fauntleroy (pilot) 26